21 Emotions

Poems on Emotions

Maha Fatima

BookLeaf Publishing

India | USA | UK

Copyright © Maha Fatima
All Rights Reserved.

This book has been self-published with all reasonable efforts taken to make the material error-free by the author. No part of this book shall be used, reproduced in any manner whatsoever without written permission from the author, except in the case of brief quotations embodied in critical articles and reviews.

The Author of this book is solely responsible and liable for its content including but not limited to the views, representations, descriptions, statements, information, opinions, and references ["Content"]. The Content of this book shall not constitute or be construed or deemed to reflect the opinion or expression of the Publisher or Editor. Neither the Publisher nor Editor endorse or approve the Content of this book or guarantee the reliability, accuracy, or completeness of the Content published herein and do not make any representations or warranties of any kind, express or implied, including but not limited to the implied warranties of merchantability, fitness for a particular purpose.

The Publisher and Editor shall not be liable whatsoever...

Made with ❤ on the BookLeaf Publishing Platform
www.bookleafpub.in
www.bookleafpub.com

Dedication

To all the people who go through various emotions in life.

Some people can express emotions easily, while some find it difficult.

Preface

21 Emotions is a collection of twenty-one poems portraying different emotions.

On my ongoing journey towards self-discovery, I came across various types of people.

Some people were good at expressing what they felt, while some found it tough.

I am grateful to meet like-minded people. It gave me the confidence to begin my journey of writing,
as I myself was someone who found it difficult to express emotions.

I hope the poems resonate with you, whether it is joy or sorrow
or through a sentence or even a single word

Acknowledgements

My gratitude to BookLeaf Publishing for giving me an opportunity to make this book a reality.
The 21-day challenge helped me push myself creatively.

I would like to thank my parents for their support.

I am sooooo grateful to my sibling, my best friend Nada, the editor for your insightful feedback and for helping me shape my words whenever I required your assistance.

And a special thanks to Mukhtar for reminding me of the importance of expressing emotions in life.

I would also like to thank the people behind my back who helped me directly and indirectly reach this level, Mr.Charan Teja, Ms.Jyotsana, Mr.Nikhil, Mr.Sundaram, Ms.Uma Madhavi and also many more I am thankful from the bottom of my heart.

Dear readers, I am very grateful for your presence in life. I hope I was able to convey and connect.

Sincere apologies for any mistakes that were made while making of this book.

1. Love

In the calmness of the night
Your smile creates a symphony in the air
It's a feeling that I have yearned for
A place where all my doubts and fears disappear

Love doesn't need to be loud
Nor does it require words
It's an understanding in the silence of our hearts

In your eyes, I can see a pool of dreams
A place where our love resides

Your warm embrace makes me feel whole and safe
I will hold on to you as long as my breath lasts

The gentle touch of love is soft like a feather if found
between the right people

2. Hate

Hate is like a flame which never dies
It lingers inside and makes the person dry
Hate kills the person inside
Even though he seems to smile on the outside

The memory of us is a bitter frost
It's a cruel reminder of what is lost
And shattered a loving heart into broken pieces

Hate grows now and poisons the soul
Where our love once bloomed

You walked away without turning, and I stayed
I hate it, that I cannot see you again
I tried to stop you
But my words went unheard, just like my love for you

Now I pick my shattered heart and crushed soul
And burn from every scar you have left me with.

3. Anger

A loud thunder roars within my chest
A fire has been ignited and it cannot be put to rest

Anger is such which cannot be controlled
There's no way someone can be calm
When there is so much injustice around

Pulsatile veins like meanders
Twisted mind-like twisters
Pounding heart-like roars of lion
Gritted teeth like roots of trees

Nothing right can be done in angst
Hence a decision needs to be made
Either I surrender myself to anger
Or start a new day

4. Happiness

Happiness is different for you and me
It is the little things that matter most to me

The warm sunshine rays in winter mornings
The bright sunshine paints the entire field of sunflowers
And they bloom like a bouquet of happiness

When you look into my eyes,
When you smile,
When you rest your head on my shoulder,
When we share about each other's day,
You hear me out when I am vulnerable, makes me happy

The laughter of children coming from the playground
Unexpected greetings from loved ones
Lightening up houses during festivities

Happiness surrounds us in the little things
We just need to pause and embrace it to enjoy

5. Sadness

Tired of trying to hide the face of sadness, By
Wearing a mask of happiness

The mask fits in perfectly as it's been years of practice by
now,
And it hasn't been noticed by any

It's easy now to hide the tears from my eyes
And just cry through my heart
Not a shed of tear, drops on the ground
Only my soul catches the drops from my sunken heart

Sitting in a dark room, I hold onto the heart that aches
Nothing can calm the heaviness in my heart
For what has already been lost cannot be brought

In the darkness, I embrace the sadness
Of my scarred heart and wait for it to heal.

6. Awkwardness

Like every morning, I stood out
For fresh air after my workout
I noticed someone staring at me
I hid at first,
then I peeked again and saw
She was the lady below my opposite flatmate

She was waving again
And this time in the evening mumbling some words
I grew tensed and unsure of what to do

I tried to open my balcony and wave her back,
Only to trip forward and
A pot of plant fell on the ground.
And an uncle shouted, and I hid
I did not come out again for the fear of the uncle,

That evening, I heard a ruckus under the building
I went out to see in the balcony,
only to find the

The watchman climbing through my balcony ladder
To handover my pjs.
I wish I could hide myself in the ground at that very
second

7. Anxiety

In the darkness of my qualm, thousands of thoughts leer
in
My mind, debating about the choices I have made and
Start creating a web of doubts
This web slowly starts tightening my ribs

I feel a prisoner in my own body
I try to scream, yet my voice reaches nobody
As my lips are stitched by thy web of my qualm

My heart feels like a ticking bomb and
I feel like bait in a webbed cocoon
Whose end is near very soon

I try to calm myself and hold my breath to stop all the
thoughts
But a slip of air passes in and again the
The whole cycle continues

8. Calmness

The ocean is still, and the air is fresh
The sky is clear blue, and the grass is luscious green

I hear no disturbance of the city traffic
Nor the chitter chatter of people
Or their hurriedness in life

It's quiet and calm
Me lying on the green grass and admiring the blue sky
I can feel the breeze touch me and pass by
And the smooth rustle of the leaves
I can hear the birds taking a flight
Flapping their wings in the breeze

It's this calmness my heart searches for which can
Only be found in the symphony of nature

I relax and take a deep breath and close my eyes
And humm into the calmness of nature
And fall asleep.

9. Awestruck

After having a bad day, I decided to take
a few snacks and cushions
and spend some time
in my favorite terrace corner

I popped some snacks and finally lay on the cushions
And my eyes fell on the stars in the sky
I was surprised, as there were hardly any clouds and, the
sky was so clear
The stars were glittering
And my bad day was turning into a happy one

Then out of nowhere
A glittery star passed with speed. Then another passed
Then another, and it continued

I couldn't believe my eyes
I was awestruck by the beauty of it
I was witnessing a meteor shower
It was a scene beyond words to describe

10. Confusion

Confusion encircles like a never-ending game
The heart needs something but the mind wants
something else
What do I do?
It's a constant battle inside me

Everything seems so unclear and twisted
There's no clarity to any of my questions
I stand lost in this confused puzzle
Just like a lost caravan in a desert

Even if I am finally sure about something
it doesn't matter,
As the opposite person is not yet certain
I need to rethink my decisions.

Caught in such a loop of confusion
I am tired of searching,
That now, I need a dictionary of clarity

11. Excitement

I can't keep my feet on the floor,
I can't feel at rest
My pulse is on a roller coaster ride
Just like my excitement

Goosebumps on my skin,
Tingling in my heart,
Eyes wide and glittering with joy

There's an eagerness to finally see the moment
I have been waiting for

I can feel my heartbeats faster
And produce fireworks inside

The rush makes me blush
I want to fly high and spread my wings and
Feel the clouds
I can't contain the excitement anymore
Inside me.

12. Horror

In the darkness of the dark, I hear whispers
I see shadows in the hallway, and I fear
The room is dead silent, and I can only hear my breath

The howling of the winds scares me
I slowly peep through the door
And decide to go to the hallway

But I dare not step into the pitch-dark alley
I tiptoed my way but stepped
Onto something sticky and gooey

I screamed at the top of my lungs
And suddenly, all the doors in the hallway opened
Masked women dressed in white marched towards me
With tears in my eyes and sweaty palms
I throw punches in the air and try to fight them

As the lights were turned on, I realized
They were my aunts in face masks!!!

13. Nostalgia

Standing in the attic, I find an old radio
There's some static
Then finally some classics are played

Closed my eyes and hummed to the tunes
And my memories rewind

I could hear the pool party when I was a kid
In a garden with my friends laughing
And water splashing
I could smell the Grilled barbeque and fries
And the voice of the adults

As the summer sun hit my face
I woke up back to reality
Dusted the old photographs and toys
And
Reminded myself
I would surely come back again
For a bit more of nostalgia, again

14. Boredom

The room is full of silence and all I hear
Is the ticking of the clock
Every second drags by like an hour
The days are already long, but the night seems
Even longer and I wait for the arrival of the dawn

Staring at the walls, I try to think of
Ways of filling the void in my life,
But nothing seems to interest
Me anymore

I yearn for the cheerfulness in my life to be back,
And try to ignite my soul again
Although there's no spark left, I try to ignite but fumble
I try again and again
And again

I had vowed to keep trying to find it till
My boredom goes and something did

Excite me one day and that day all the grey colors in my
life
Turned to solid hues.

15. Disappointment

My heart had some hope,
But every time I tried to speak to you
You would push me away
And I would crumble

I kept trying to rebuild the castle of hopes
With my burnt hands
But never knew, you were That flame who could even
Burn the sand and turn it into Ashes with just your
words

You tried every possible way to put me down
You shut my mouth, by pointing out that,
I am such a disappointment.
You were embarrassed, being seen out with me.

You kept putting me down
At the very time, I needed you the most.
But it was you, who were a disappointment
I am glad I understood at least later than never

16. Contentment

Sitting in the garden and watching the sunrise
It had been the most beautiful
And peaceful event I was able to do throughout the week

It's so true that no amount of luxury can fill up the heart
It's just pure greed
Contentment is like the flower that blooms
While living in the present

This satisfaction can only be found when we
Live life not for the rush or riches but
For happiness, love and peace

It lies in the simple things
Of life

17. Grief

It was only yesterday when you came into my life
As our eyes met, there felt an instant connection
It felt like, we could read each other

Wish there was a way to bring you back
Or at the least I could just get a peek of you, Playing in
the clouds
But it is too late now, you are gone too early

Although you are free from the pain
My tears just don't stop when I hear your name
I miss your tiny little paws
Kneading bread and biscuits like my mini baker
I miss your sweet little meows
Because you wanted to me hold you in my arms
I miss those cute boba eyes
Who would only sleep when I would hug and cuddle you
to sleep

I wish we had more time together

Forgive me for not seeing you when you closed your
eyes forever
I wasn't brave enough to see you so
I still haven't overcome your loss my little one

18. Hope

Hope is a beautiful yet a powerful rope of anticipation
Which guides someone in the darkest shadows of their
doubts

Without hope, it would have been difficult
To reach goals in our life
To seek out new adventures
To take risks in life

It's that little corner in our heart where
You have the willingness to move forward
And not give up on life

Hope is something where you
look forward to another sunrise

It would mean a lot to someone, if
Just One person shows a little ray of hope.
You may never know when the goodness will return to
you!

19. Failure

I have tried my best to reach not just yours but
everybody's expectations
But I kept falling harder every time on the cold hard
surface

I get up every time and try to work even harder after
each failure,
But nothing works out and it's very tiring.
More than the failure, I am tired of your harsh and cruel
words
And how you fail to understand me

The irony of life is that the people closest
Are the ones who fail to understand and leave you
Alone during the time of failure
And it reveals their true colors

I can't seem to face myself after so many failed attempts
As every scar reminds me of each attempt I have tried

But still, I try not to give up and hold myself strong
And today I walk out of the door to give another
attempt,
But this time it is to reach my expectations

20. Desire

My desire is:

To see your happiness
To see you smile again
To see you live your life to the fullest

To enjoy every moment in life and
Not care what anybody thinks,
To not come under the pressure of society or peers

To stay healthy and take care of your body
Concentrate not just on the physical but also
On mental and emotional well-being

To share your emotions and feelings
and not suffocate

To give a chance to people in life
and trust them

To understand life is full of ups and downs.
And life is unplanned
So, stop waiting for the right time
And some risks are worth taking

If someone is giving you their hand do, consider..........
Life is filled with surprises

21. Romance

Under the moonlight and glittering stars
We are lost in each other's gaze
A sudden gust of cold air forces us to embrace each other
I blush and keep my head on your chest

You hold my hand and we sway to the tune of the
rustling leaves
It felt like only we both could hear the song being played
We both continued to sway
I could hear your heartbeats getting fast as we got closer
We twirl and twirl and sway and twirl and our eyes lock
We stood there for what looked like forever

In my heart, I never wanted to leave you and
Embrace you forever
The clouds might have heard my thoughts and
Covered the moon
As I came closer to hug you, but you turned quickly
And my lips brushed against yours
And the rest is anticipated.....

www.ingramcontent.com/pod-product-compliance
Lightning Source LLC
LaVergne TN
LVHW021328200726
843509LV00014B/2437